SPORTS GIRL

COMPETITIVE
FASTPITCH SOFTBALL
FOR GIRLS

ANN WESLEY

the rosen publishing group's
rosen central

To Amy most of all and to Velma, Jack, Sally, and Donna for encouragement and support in everything.

Published in 2001 by The Rosen Publishing Group, Inc.
29 East 21st Street, New York, NY 10010

Library of Congress Cataloging-in-Publication Data

Wesley, Ann
Competitive fastpitch softball for girls / by Ann Wesley. — 1st ed.
p. cm. — (SportsGirl)
Includes bibliographical references and index.
ISBN 0-8239-3409-8
1. Softball for women. I. Title. II. Series.
GV881.3 .W47 2001
796.357'8—dc21

00-012063

Manufactured in the United States of America

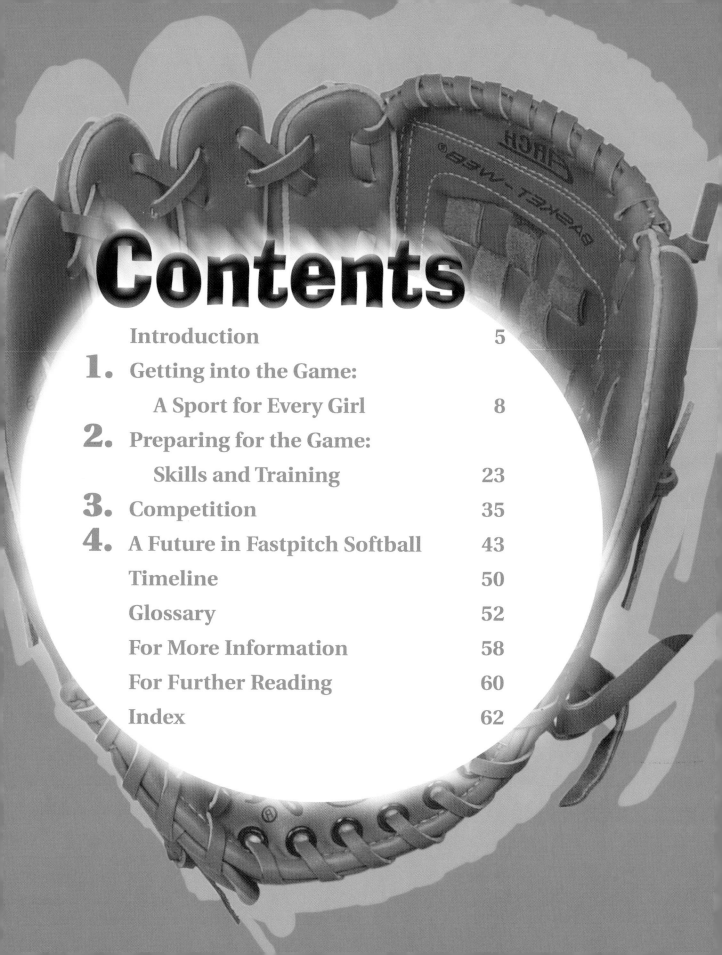

Contents

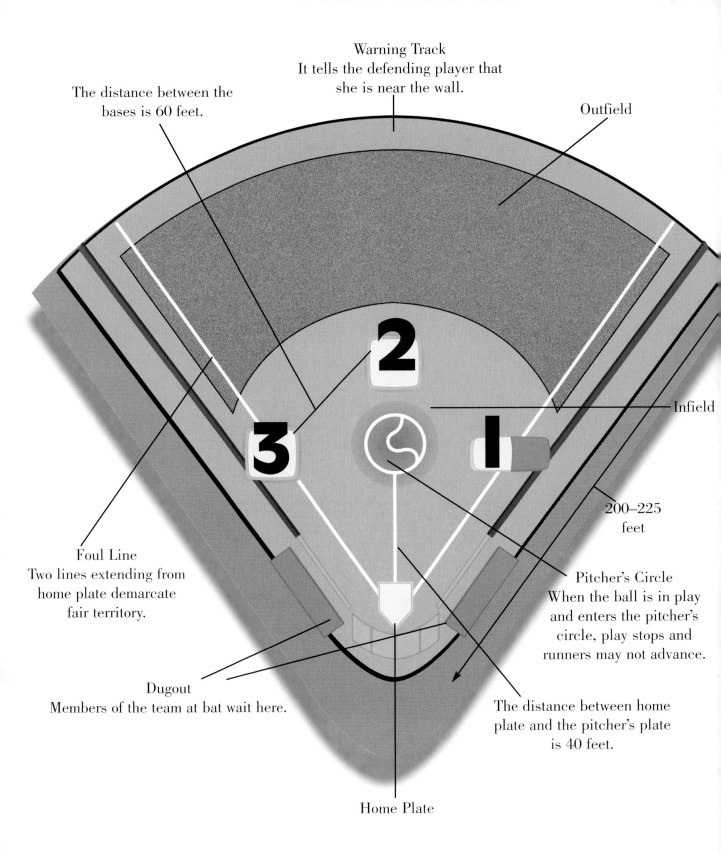

Warning Track
It tells the defending player that
she is near the wall.

The distance between the
bases is 60 feet.

Outfield

Infield

200–225
feet

Pitcher's Circle
When the ball is in play
and enters the pitcher's
circle, play stops and
runners may not advance.

Foul Line
Two lines extending from
home plate demarcate
fair territory.

Dugout
Members of the team at bat wait here.

The distance between home
plate and the pitcher's plate
is 40 feet.

Home Plate

Introduction

When a girl steps into the batter's box and locks eyes with the pitcher, both have the same thought: "I want to beat her." The pitcher wants to throw the ball with such speed or accuracy that the batter is unable to make contact. The batter wants her timing to be perfect so she can hit the ball and feel the exhilarating vibration of the bat as she takes off sprinting for first base. To hear the fans cheer, to help the team, to know you have done your best, is nothing less than euphoric. But this fiercely competitive spirit was not the intent of the game's promoters back in the 1920s and 1930s, when the sport was promoted to girls because of its "softness."

The first softball game, dating back to 1887, didn't even involve a ball, but rather was played by a group of college men throwing a boxing glove and hitting it with a stick. It caught on, developed, and was played by local teams and in firehouses. At one time the

Since softball was introduced in the 1930s, girls have found ways to make it more competitive.

game was referred to as kitten ball. In the 1930s it became more organized and a tournament was scheduled in conjunction with the 1933 Chicago World's Fair. Several dozen teams participated, in divisions including fastball, slowball, and women. At that time, the ball was fourteen inches in diameter and play was fairly tame.

In the 1930s, baseball was banned on women's high school and college campuses, and physical education instructors urged girls to play softball as a way to steer them away from sports in which the physical demands were thought to be too much for girls. Softball used a ball larger than a baseball and was slower than other games—something thought to be more appropriate for females. It didn't take long however, for girls to find ways to make the sport more competitive and prove they could handle more strenuous activity. Playing in community leagues, women pushed the game to new heights in the 1940s, when its popularity extended from coast to coast and American women participated in international competition.

Because they weren't allowed to participate in Little League baseball, many girls turned to softball. With the benefits of Title IX in 1972—the law that gives girls and boys equal sports opportunities in federally funded schools—girls began to get more funding for sports programs in high schools and colleges, and softball became more competitive.

In 1982, the National Collegiate Athletic Association (NCAA) held the first Women's College World Series, which is now the national college championship for softball.

Today, many girls are attracted to softball because of its physical challenges—hitting, running, sliding, diving for balls. Any "soft" element of the game has been eliminated. Girls get dirty, sweaty, scraped, bruised, and blistered.

And opportunities to play abound. Girls can play softball from just past the age of toddler well into retirement. There are organized leagues that extend from community groups to school teams, college competition, national amateur travel leagues, the Olympic team, and even a professional league. Nearly every town and city, no matter how rural or urban, supports softball leagues.

This book will introduce some of the basics of the game, the enjoyment the sport provides its participants, and the opportunities that lie ahead for those interested in seriously pursuing softball.

1

Getting into the Game: A Sport for Every Girl

With many sports, girls may feel they don't have a chance to excel if they aren't extremely tall, thin, or athletically built, or didn't begin mastering the game at a very early age. Softball, however, is one of the few sports that anyone can play and have a good chance of finding success in—regardless of body type or when she started playing.

"Anyone with good hand-eye coordination can play," says John Carroll, the CEO of the Women's Professional Softball League. "You don't have to be six feet six. In this game you don't have to be big to play. This game appeals to a broader base of participation."

Many of the top softball players don't fit a traditional athletic body type. Players can be short, tall, average, slim, or even chunky and still be good. In fact, for some positions, such as catcher, a bigger, sturdier body can be an advantage. (When a runner is sliding in to home plate and needs to get past a crouching catcher, sometimes a bigger body enables the catcher to hold her ground more easily.) In this game, a desire to win and willingness to work hard are often bigger assets than weight or height.

Lisa Fernandez, considered one of the best pitchers ever in fastpitch softball, stands only five feet six and has an average build. Fernandez was once told she couldn't play softball because her arms were too short. But her desire to play and commitment to hard work helped her become not only one of the best college players, but also one of the best international players ever.

Softball can also be learned relatively quickly, though it may take years of practice to reach the top levels. The 2000 College World Series is a perfect example of that. Several of the players on the Southern Mississippi University (SMU) team didn't even play fastpitch softball until they reached college. The basic athleticism of the players enabled them to pick up the game quickly and play on an elite level.

Slowpitch: A Different Game

In slowpitch softball, the ball is pitched underhand without much speed and is easy to hit. The game's focus is primarily offense and scores often run into the teens. Because most balls are hit into play, the game includes ten defensive players instead of the nine found in fastpitch softball. Slowpitch softball is primarily a recreational sport played in community leagues. Base stealing is not allowed, nor is bunting.

Getting Started

Most players begin learning the game in slowpitch leagues to master fielding, hitting, and base running, and then advance to fastpitch leagues when they become more serious about the sport. Fastpitch softball involves more strategy, including a variety of pitches, base stealing, and bunting.

The basic rules of fastpitch softball are very similar to baseball. The game is divided into innings in which each team has one offensive and one defensive cycle. Each part of the cycle consists of three outs. Some of the major differences between fastpitch softball and baseball are:

- A softball game is seven innings long, and a baseball game consists of nine innings.

Softball is played on a dirt infield and baseball has a grass infield. The surface of the infield can affect how the ball moves.

Softball has a flat pitching mound and baseball has a raised mound. In softball the pitch is delivered under-hand while baseball involves an overhand throw.

The softball is eleven inches in circumference in most leagues.

The distance from home plate to the pitcher's mound is shorter in softball. The pitcher stands forty-three feet from home plate in softball. In baseball, the pitcher is sixty feet six inches from the plate. However, the speed at which the ball arrives at home plate can at times be faster and thus harder to hit in softball than in baseball. While high school pitchers may hurl at 50 to 60 mph, the top pitchers in the professional leagues can pitch at 70 mph or more. With the shorter distance to the plate, many compare that pitch to baseball's fastball moving at 90 to 100 mph.

Equipment

In order to begin playing softball, there is some basic equipment each girl will need. With the growth of the game, many top

Softball requires equipment such as a ball, glove, and bat. Catchers need additional safety equipment such as a helmet, chest protector, and shin guards.

companies are making softball equipment specifically for girls and some national players even endorse specific lines named after them. First there is the ball, and though each girl may have her own for private practice, it isn't necessary. Often a team will share several bats, but as a girl advances in the game, she may want her own bat. Each player will need her own glove. Some girls prefer to wear a batting glove, but one isn't required. Baseball or softball cleats are needed and are available at most athletic shoe stores. Catchers will need additional safety equipment. When batting, a player will need to wear a batting helmet, but the team generally provides several which are shared.

Bats

To judge the proper length of bat you need, stand in place and put the bat next to you with the barrel end on the floor. If the handle hits just at your wrist, it is the correct length. If the handle is at your palm, fingers, or lower, it will be too short. If it extends up your arm, it will be too long. Finding the correct weight is a matter of personal preference and ability. Hitters have more power with a heavier bat, but only if they have the strength to swing the bat with balance and appropriate speed. The advantage of owning your own bat is that you can practice your swing during your free time and become a better hitter.

Gloves

Each player on defense will need a glove, or mitt, to catch the ball. Catchers use a special, thicker glove designed as a target and constructed to allow girls to catch balls thrown hard and fast. Outfielders tend to prefer gloves with large, long fingers which allow them to capture balls more easily, while infielders prefer gloves with shorter fingers that allow them to remove and throw the ball faster. The glove should fit comfortably and not be too large for the girl's hand.

Catching Equipment

The catcher needs the most equipment in order to protect herself from hard-thrown balls that may get away from her. A catcher should wear a well-fitted mask along with a throat protector, a helmet, a chest protector, and shin guards. She should wear this equipment at all times when behind the plate.

Play Ball: Positions

After the proper equipment is purchased and broken in, and the basics of the game are understood, it's time to play. While softball is easy to understand, mastering the skills needed to play well takes time and practice.

The speed of the game requires that players have quick reflexes, especially the players in the infield, who are going to have fast pitches hit directly toward them. There are six defensive positions in the infield: the pitcher and catcher who make up what is called the battery, first base, second base, shortstop, and third base. In the outfield there are three players: a left fielder, a center fielder, and a right fielder.

Pitcher and Catcher

Players interested in being a pitcher or catcher need to have good endurance because they are involved in every defensive play and also take turns at bat on offense. In addition to being strong athletes, these two players need an extra degree of mental toughness. If the pitcher walks a player or throws a bad pitch, she can't afford to get rattled or upset. That can result in more bad pitches. She must have the

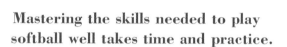

Mastering the skills needed to play softball well takes time and practice.

ability to keep her focus on every throw. The catcher must lead the infield. Infielders face the catcher during the game and the team takes direction from her. She must make sure everyone knows what to expect on each play and she must keep her pitcher focused.

The pitcher generally dictates the game. A strong pitcher can stop a good hitter. The fewer times the ball is hit, the fewer chances the opponent has to score. If the pitcher is getting the

The catcher needs to be a strong athlete and have good endurance because she is involved in every defensive play.

ball in the strike zone and throwing hitters out, the opponent goes down fast. A good pitcher, controlling the other team, can give her teammates confidence and make them more secure at bat, knowing the other team will have a hard time scoring. A player who can handle or enjoys pressure and controlling the game makes a good pitcher.

Pitcher Lisa Fernandez often stresses the importance of brainpower over athleticism. "I'm not your prototypical athlete. I'm not exceptionally fast or overly powerful. I make up for it by using technique and trying to be smarter."

Complementing the pitcher is the catcher, the team leader. The catcher will get dirty and can get knocked down on plays but she must remain composed at all times. She is responsible for vocally commanding the team throughout the game. She must have very good hand-eye coordination, be flexible, and have an arm strong and accurate enough to throw from behind the plate to any of the bases.

To an extent, the catcher must know every infielder's responsibility and be ready to yell it out as the ball is put in play. She must keep the team informed of how many outs there are and what the count is on each play, and she must guide the pitcher on every throw. The catcher generally sends signals to the pitcher dictating what type of pitch to throw. She must watch base runners and try to throw them out when a steal is attempted. She also calls the action on a bunt. All of this is in addition to catching every pitch and guarding home plate to prevent runners from scoring.

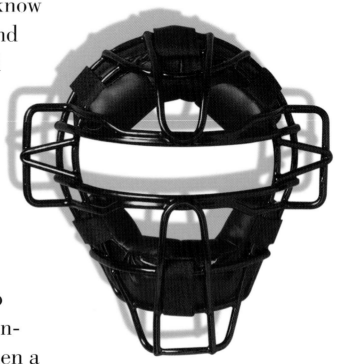

A catcher should wear a well-fitted mask to protect herself from hard-thrown balls.

Girls interested in playing catcher have to be outgoing and assertive. They can't be shy about telling other people what to do. Sometimes girls possess athletic skills but shyness or a demure personality keeps them from being an effective catcher. Learning to speak up and take control is sometimes the hardest aspect of being a good catcher.

Basemen and Shortstop

The remaining infield players must have good reflexes in order to catch fast-moving balls, tag bases, and throw the ball to another fielder.

The girl playing first base is often among the tallest players on the team. She needs to provide a big target for other infielders to throw to. She also must be able to keep a foot on first base and stretch her body as far as possible toward the other bases when receiving a throw. This person must possess excellent catching skills and be reliable. All the other infielders will be throwing the ball to first base regularly. Often the balls are thrown so quickly they may not be perfectly accurate. A good athlete at first base will find ways to grab bad throws and make the outs. Her ability to get the out at first base stops any possibility of runners moving into scoring position.

Girls playing second base and shortstop are known as middle infielders. Generally, they are the most agile players on the team because they have to cover and control the largest portion of the infield. The person playing second stands a few feet from the base on the first base side. The shortstop stands between second base and third base. These two players are called on to cover their positions, make double plays, stop steals, and serve as the cutoff for outfielders throwing the ball. Quick reflexes are very important for second base and shortstop. When the ball is hit between first and second base, the girl playing second base gets the ball and the shortstop moves over to cover the base. When the ball is hit between second and third, the girl playing shortstop gets the ball and the girl playing second covers the base. The shortstop may also have to move to cover third base, if that fielder moves in to field a bunt or moves out to catch a fly ball.

Infielders must be agile in order to cover the bases and keep runners from moving into scoring position.

Third base is often called the hot spot or hot corner. Balls reach this position very fast and the defensive player has little time to react. She must be able to snag these hits out of the air and be equally able to charge the plate to pick up a bunt and fire it to first base. This player should be someone who is aggressive, smart, and fast.

Outfield

Beyond the infield, the left, center, and right fielders are responsible for catching fly balls, picking up grounders, and getting the ball back to the infield as quickly and accurately as possible. They must make good judgements when the ball is hit, deciding in a split second where the ball is going so they can quickly move to catch it. Fielders must back each other up and communicate well to avoid colliding or letting the ball drop between them when two players are moving toward the same ball and looking up rather than at each other. Outfielders have more time to react to the ball than infielders, but unless the ball is hit exactly to them, they must move quickly to get to it and make the out. Once the ball is caught, the fielder must get it to the infield quickly to make a double play or stop runners from advancing.

Offense

On offense, all nine defensive players may bat or a designated hitter may bat for one offensive player. Each team establishes a batting order before the game starts and follows it throughout the game.

As with fielding, quick reflexes are essential in hitting. With balls moving toward the plate at 50 to 70 mph, the hitter has no more than a second to eye it, decide where it is going, move the bat into position, and swing to send the ball back onto the field. Hitting can be the most difficult act in the sport, but is often the most fun and popular. Being a top hitter takes an extraordinary amount of practice and work. When a batter steps in the box (the area on the right or left side of the plate measuring three feet wide by seven feet long) she must be ready to hit. Good hitters will possess as many different options of moving the ball as a good pitcher. Often the coach will tell a player how or where to try to place the ball before she hits in order to move players already on the bases. The hitter and pitcher face off in the ultimate duel. When the hitter wins, she or a teammate safely reaches base. When the pitcher wins, they do not. While home runs are the glory hits in softball, they aren't the goal of each turn at bat. It is equally important to have runners on the bases in order to score more runs.

Sometimes, a hitter is asked to stand in the batter's box and not swing the bat. If a pitcher is struggling to get the ball in the strike zone, the coach will tell the hitter to hold off swinging and try to draw a walk. Knowing when the pitch is not going to be in the strike zone can be as valuable as being a home run slugger. Getting on base gives your team more opportunities to score and puts more pressure on the defensive team because they then have to work to get the next batter out and keep you from advancing. In other situations, batters may be asked to put the ball into play in an area that is likely to lead to an out. This is called a sacrifice. The defense will often get the batter out but another base runner will have the opportunity to score or advance toward scoring. Fly balls to the outfield are often sacrifice hits, allowing a fast runner to advance from one base to the next after the ball is caught but before it is thrown back to the infield. Bunting, a short hit that moves only a few feet from home plate, is also frequently used as a way to sacrifice, although a good bunt by a fast runner can often lead to the batter and base runner advancing safely.

One of the most important aspects of hitting is confidence. Players must approach the plate believing they can hit the ball and unafraid of the pitcher. If a batter has not been hitting successfully, she may question her ability, and when that is combined with chatter from the catcher, it is easy for concentration to be lost. The hitter who can block out distractions and focus her complete attention on the pitch has a good chance of making contact. Going to the plate with the intention of making contact with the ball leads to success.

2 Preparing for the Game: Skills and Training

Softball players will all have a preferred position, but many players will become versatile enough to play several different positions. When playing the game, each player may have to use the skills of different positions to execute a play. For example, outfielders will primarily need to know how to catch fly balls, but that doesn't mean infielders shouldn't master this skill as well. Infielders will need to catch pop ups—balls hit straight up that don't travel past the infield. They also will need to catch the short fly—a fly ball that goes just past the infield, but is easier for the infielder to handle than for an outfielder. The following are some of the most common plays and how to deal with them—things all players should know.

When going after a fly ball, catch the ball
with your arms and glove extended upward.

Fly Balls

Sometimes, the hardest part of catching a fly ball is judging where it will land and knowing in which direction to move to catch it. A common mistake is to start running to the ball the instant it is hit. Players should wait for just enough time to pass to determine if the ball is going to come down in front of or behind them. Moving too soon in the wrong direction causes the player to have to make up too much distance to get to the ball and often results in missing the catch. When the player knows in which direction to move to make the catch, it is important that she maintain eye contact with the ball and call out her intent to catch it to other players. This will prevent collisions between two players going for the same ball.

When making the fly ball catch, the ball should come down just in front of you. Catch the ball with your arms and glove extended up—the fingers of the glove should be pointing upward and the palm of the glove facing away from you. When the ball is in the glove, bring the glove down and in toward the chest to keep from dropping the ball. If runners are on base, you should then throw as fast and accurately as possible to the appropriate base or to your cutoff, a fielder who will relay the ball to the proper base. When a ball is caught deep in the outfield, another player accepts the throw halfway to the base and relays it on. She is the cutoff. When making a throw, it is important to keep the ball level or low. High arching throws from the outfield to the infield waste time.

If a short fly is hit and you are running forward from the outfield to catch it, you will change the position of the glove to catch the ball below your waist. In these cases, the glove should be turned over with the back facing the ground and the palm facing up. You should guide the ball in with your throwing hand and then quickly remove it to throw the ball to the infield. The same action should be taken for grounders coming into the outfield. Use both hands to catch the ball and bring it safely into the glove.

The best way to learn to catch fly balls is practice. One of the most common drills for learning this skill is to position girls in the outfield and have a coach hit fly balls to them, calling out the name of the girl responsible for catching each ball. Frequently during practice, one coach will work with infielders and another will use the outfield space to hit fly balls. When the full team is not practicing, two players can work together on catching fly balls by standing far apart and throwing high balls to each other.

Catching in the Infield

Infielders must know how to catch fly balls, but must also catch a variety of other hits and must react more quickly in order to cover their base or catch and throw a runner out on another base. Infielders must work on receiving balls without bobbling them and must know how to throw quickly and accurately. Quick reflexes are essential. In addition to fly balls, some hitters will send the ball back as a line drive—a ball hit between waist and head height. Infielders must field line drives, as well as ground balls and bunts.

When catching a ground ball, the fielder should lower the whole glove to the ground. The body should be positioned in front of the ball and the player should move low to it. Standing with feet apart, bending only at the waist can sometimes result in the embarrassing situation of having the ball roll through the legs. As with any catch, watch the ball all the way into the glove. The player should only move toward the rolling grounder if it is a slow roller or a bunt. Otherwise, leading the play with the glove down should give plenty of time to scoop the ball up and throw it to the appropriate base. What's important to remember is that even if the ball is dropped, if a player maintains composure, it can be quickly retrieved and the out can often still be made.

The more times girls catch and throw balls, the more comfortable they will become with fielding. The most basic and common drill begins with girls standing several feet apart throwing the ball to each other. After several successful catches they each back up and throw the ball harder and farther. As the drill continues, girls can throw different types of balls to practice different fielding techniques— grounders, high flies, pop ups, etc. This is continued until the ball is being thrown the distance of bases. The drill allows girls to warm up before games and can help prevent arm injuries.

The Bunt

One play every girl in fastpitch softball must learn is the bunt. The bunt is one of the most strategic hits. It consists of the batter slapping or tapping the ball down so that it moves only a few feet from home plate. Any time there is a runner on base and zero or one out, a bunt can be expected. It is used to move the runner to the next base. Infielders generally will know when a batter is going to bunt by the way she holds the bat. Rather than holding it at the knob end with the bat barrel above the shoulders, a bunter will put one hand on the grip and the other on the barrel and hold it across her body so she can push it at a pitch.

When a bunt is shown, the fielders at first and third base should move in about halfway to the plate, close to the foul line. The second baseman will need to cover first base and the shortstop will cover second or third base depending on where the runners are and which player rushes in to field the bunt. The catcher will be the leader in fielding the bunt but the pitcher should be prepared to rush in as well. When the bunt is hit in fair territory, the catcher will play it if it is within reach. If it is hit or rolls a bit farther, the catcher will direct the play by calling out which base the fielder should throw to.

As with every aspect of softball, it takes a lot of practice to learn to hit and defend the bunt. Early on, coaches can begin by positioning the fielders and hitting bunt after bunt to show the girls the movement of the bat. Later, runners can be positioned

The underhand circular motion used in fastpitch softball may seem unnatural, but it does not hurt and is not uncomfortable.

on bases and the coach can hit bunts and allow fielders to play the ball. A considerable amount of time should be spent at each practice learning to defend against the bunt.

Pitching

In order for fielders to use their skills, the ball must be put into play during a game. That's where the pitcher comes in. A good pitcher can control the tempo of the game. A nervous pitcher or girl struggling to find her mark can start walking batters and the game can quickly get out of control.

Pitching is perhaps the most difficult position to learn and will take more practice than other positions. It is recommended that a girl learning to pitch partner with someone who has mastered the skill or work with an experienced pitching coach who can help her learn correct form and technique. While the underhand circular motion used in fastpitch softball may seem unnatural, quite the opposite is true. Thrown correctly, the motion does not hurt and is not uncomfortable. Once a girl masters the basics, though, her work has just begun. From there, she will learn to throw a variety of different pitches at different speeds and place the pitch exactly where the hitters don't want it.

Understanding the basics of the pitch will help a pitcher get started. Then, as with every position, it's on to hours on the practice field. In fastpitch softball, the pitcher holds the ball with her fingers, not in the palm of her hand. The grip on the ball should be with two or three fingers and should be firm but not too tight. When making the pitch, the arm should be relaxed through the circular motion and then snap or act like a whip to throw the pitch, with the pitcher striving for strong acceleration as the arm moves through the downward motion of the arch. As the ball is released, the pitcher will step with the pitch, but she must be sure not to lunge. The step should be made straight toward the plate. With the step, the weight must be kept back until the wrist snaps and the pitch is released. At that point, all power is thrust forward. It is important to remember that the whole body is used in the "windmill" pitch. The pitch is delivered in one motion. The ball is released

Every softball player should master hitting because each player takes a turn at bat.

when the arm comes down to the hip. The wrist snaps and the ball is hurled off the fingers toward the plate.

When learning to pitch, girls should first spend time practicing the motion and step without the ball. When they become comfortable with the circle, they can add the ball and practice the snap. Practicing the motion in front of a mirror (without throwing the ball) is a good way for a girl to see her mechanics. After the motion is learned, pitchers can practice against a backstop marked with a strike zone or a pitching net. Finally, after a girl learns to put the ball across the plate on a regular basis, she can begin work with a catcher and start learning to throw pitches at different angles, with different degrees of spin, speed, and placement. Meredith Shackleford, a high school pitcher who went undefeated her freshman and sophomore years, says, "I have played almost every position and the outfield. I think that every position has its difficulties. The hardest for me has always been pitching. It is the one I have put the most work into and until recently have never been satisfied with my

When gripping the bat, your hands should be close together and within three inches of the knob of the bat.

performance. I still have a lot of work to do and will continue to work hard."

Hitting

If pitching is the hardest softball skill to master, hitting is second. Hitting is a skill every player needs to master because everyone takes a turn at bat. And like every other skill, good hitting takes practice. A girl who owns her own bat can spend much more time practicing, learning her grip, and becoming comfortable with her swing. A girl can practice her swing just about anywhere— as long as it's a place where she doesn't have to worry about breaking anything!

The process of hitting begins with the correct grip. Your hands should be positioned close together and generally within three inches from the knob of the bat. The exact placement on the grip depends on each person's comfort level. The fingers should be relaxed when holding the bat—they will tighten automatically when the swing begins. The batter should stand with her feet shoulder-width apart. The knees should be slightly bent and the weight should be on the balls of the feet. Spectators will often see batters spend a considerable amount of time kicking dirt in the batter's box. This is how a batter makes sure the dirt is even under her feet. Where a girl stands in the batter's box may vary but generally, batters line their back foot up with the back of home plate.

Wherever you stand, the important thing is to make sure you are able to extend the bat over the entire plate. You should be far enough away from the plate to hit a pitch on the inside and close enough to hit the outside pitches when your arms are extended.

Batters should hold the bat just off their shoulders with the arms relaxed in an upside down "V." When the pitch comes in, the batter must keep constant eye contact with the ball and stride into it as it is hit. The front foot and leg will rise up and step into the pitch as the bat swings over the plate. The batter does not move forward as soon as the stride begins, but rather moves with the contact. Shifting the weight too soon will result in a loss of power on the swing. The object of the swing is to keep it level so that your arms and bat form a straight line at the point of contact. The more a girl practices the swing motion all the way through, the better she will be at hitting. Practicing the swing without a ball teaches the muscles and body the motion so that in a game situation, you can focus on watching the ball instead of thinking about your hitting motion.

Many players at all levels use a hitting T to practice their swing. A hitting T is a stand that the ball sits on. It enables the batter to focus on her swing instead of on the motion of the incoming ball. This allows her to hit the ball from a stationery position and focus on body movement. The direction the ball moves will quickly show errors in stance and swing. For example, if the ball is popping straight up, the player is likely dropping her shoulder and swinging up. If a girl is hitting balls that fall directly to the ground and roll, she is probably rolling her wrists rather than swinging through the pitch.

One of the most common drills in fastpitch softball is a short game known as pepper. In the drill, one person hits with four or five fielders standing about twenty feet away. The first fielder tosses the ball to the hitter and she hits it with a half swing. The next fielder then tosses the ball in and it continues. The object is to get the batter to hit a series of quick tosses to develop better hand-eye coordination. The batter is required to hit ground balls back to the fielders. If she hits a fly, she is out and the players rotate positions.

Fastpitch softball is a strategic game with nuances that can only be learned by doing. Once the basics of hitting and fielding are learned, girls will begin to learn base-running strategies, base stealing, sliding, place hitting, and various defensive strategies. The game then becomes as much of a mental challenge as a physical challenge, with the team that uses the best strategy and most efficient execution of skills likely to come out on top.

3 Competition

In sports, everyone wants to win. There's nothing like the feeling of trying hard and coming out on top. But it's not the only good feeling associated with sports. Whether playing in the backyard or training for a profession, if you don't enjoy what you're doing, what's the point of doing it? The feeling of success and enjoyment can come from improvement, from working hard, and from camaraderie with friends. Winning is the bonus.

"Have fun. Don't get so serious at such a young age. Parents and coaches are so focused on scholarships that it takes the fun out of the game. We should enjoy the game for what it is." That's the advice of Jennifer Brundage, U.S. Olympic team member and University of Michigan assistant coach.

Profile: Dot Richardson

Dot Richardson has lived the softball dream.

Though she's won every major award her sport offers, Richardson's career hasn't been flawless. But that's what makes her an even better player. From the time she was ten years old and had to pretend to be a boy to play baseball, to the Summer Olympics of 2000, when she helped the United States overcome three straight losses to win the gold, Richardson has succeeded because she worked hard and put team before self.

After giving up the notion of playing the boys' game, Richardson focused on fastpitch softball and went to UCLA, where she was a four-time NCAA All-America player. While pursuing a medical degree, Dot went on to become the NCAA Player of the Decade for the 1980s, was captain of the gold-medal 1996 Olympic team, and earned a second gold medal in the 2000 Olympics at the age of thirty-eight.

Athletes don't stay on top forever. After the 1996 Olympics, the U.S. national selection committee seemed to think Dr. Dot's career was over. She was dropped from the team and forced to try out for the national team in 1998. Competing against younger, stronger athletes who played year round, while she worked as a high-profile orthopedic surgeon, Richardson had to go through tryouts for a full year before she was selected, and then it was with the condition that she give up her shortstop position and play second base.

Richardson agreed to the switch and proved to the committee and the world how hard work and persistence pay off.

"I've been through the rejection and disappointment and wanting something so badly," she said. "For me, my passion for the sport of softball has been able to keep me at this level."

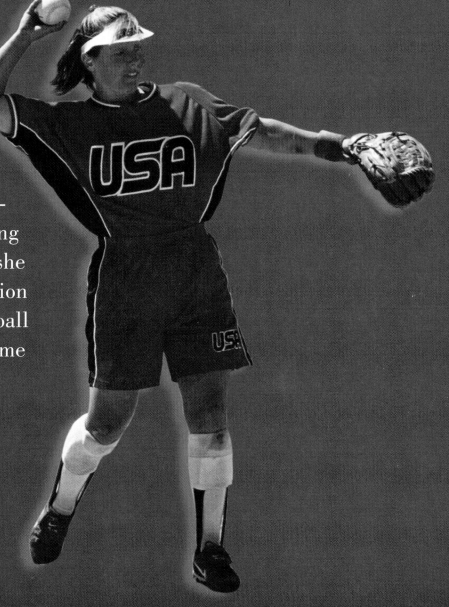

Dee Dee Weiman, a pitcher in the Women's Professional Softball League and an alternate on the 1996 Olympic team, considers softball to be one of the loves of her life. But she emphasizes that team unity and having fun with the sport are more important than being a star. "Playing in a professional league is the first real happiness I've had in softball for a long time," she said after her first season in 1997. "I play because I love it and it's fun. Playing here is not the same as college or trying to make the Olympic team, where the pressure was so intense it wasn't fun. I made the Olympics as an alternate. It was nice to know I was good enough to make that team, but I wasn't really happy. This is a wonderful family atmosphere where everyone is involved and everyone gets along," she said.

Being part of a sports team is about more than winning a trophy or praise and adoration from schoolmates. While any team is going to have some players who are better than others, the old saying holds that there is no "I" in team. One or two superstars cannot carry a whole team. In fastpitch softball, it takes all players to make a team successful. This is equally true when playing offense or defense. Maybe one player is a home-run hitter. But if other members of the team aren't capable of getting on base, drawing a walk, and moving around the base path, the team likely will lose. On defense, the pitcher and catcher may receive the most attention, but when the ball is put in play, it takes all fielders playing their positions well to get the outs and move the game forward.

In fastpitch softball, all of the players must work hard to make a team successful.

Trina Valencia started playing the game when she was eight years old on a team her mother coached. She stayed with the sport through college and learned, among other things, the thrill of being part of a team.

"I just love it. I could never do an individual sport. Just being on the team and knowing that everyone is there to accomplish something together is what I like. The competition, the situations you get into and have to get out of, that makes me feel really good," she said.

Part of being on a team means playing your role and understanding that everyone contributes. Rarely will a coach tell a player, "I want you to hit a home run" when the girl steps up to bat. Instead, the players will often be told, "We need base runners. Just a hit, we need base runners." Hitters stand a better chance of getting on base if they try to get a hit rather than trying to smash the ball out of the park. Many games are won by the team that consistently hits the ball and works as a team advancing around the bases to home plate.

Just as hitters help the team by advancing runners, fielders have to work as a unit to keep an opponent from scoring. Take the example of a pitch thrown a bit off the mark that gets by the catcher. Working as a team, the pitcher immediately rushes the plate where the catcher throws her the ball from the spot where the ball landed. By working as a unit, the pitcher is able to stop the runner at third base from scoring. Sometimes, it takes the effort of the whole team to make a play, including those sitting on the bench in the dugout. In one tournament game, a runner at first base stole second. On the next pitch, she attempted to steal third. The catcher missed the leadoff and tossed the ball back to the pitcher. Other teammates, however, were more alert, and several girls in the dugout called the play to the pitcher. She was then able to quickly throw to third just in time to have the sliding runner tagged out. Without the effort of the whole team, the runner would have reached third base safely.

Communication between team members on and off the field is crucial to success in softball. When a ball is hit, two or more fielders may move toward it at the same time. Without good communication, the girls will either collide and possibly get hurt, or they will both stop, assuming the other will make the play, and the ball may drop between them.

Mental Toughness

Much emphasis is placed on developing the physical skills needed to play ball, but coaches will quickly admit that the mental game is the hardest to teach and the most important element in sports. Being mentally strong means knowing where the ball should go, paying attention, working together, listening to instructions, and executing plays as taught. It means staying composed when things don't go as you hoped and focusing on the task at hand rather than dwelling on a missed play.

At a high school game in Indiana, after a player struck out, ending the inning for her team, she threw her helmet in the dugout, yelled, and kicked the fence before taking her position on the field at third base. On the first hit, she bobbled the ball, picked it up, and threw it to first base. The ball went sailing over the head of her teammate who was waiting to make the out. Mentally, the third baseman was still focused on her batting errors when her team took the field. Her failure to focus compounded her offensive mistake.

On another play, the second baseman dropped a line drive but quickly picked it up and threw it to first in plenty of time for the out to be made. The girl at second didn't receive a reprimand from her coach, but rather was complimented for staying with the play and focusing to get the out.

During the game the coach told the team, "I don't care if you make a mistake. Everyone is going to make mistakes. You've just got to shake them off and put the hammer down. Play to win and keep your head in the game."

On another field on a hot August day, a team was leading 2-0 in the fifth inning when the coach called time out and huddled the team together. Rather than complimenting the players for their effort, he seriously scolded them for relaxing and losing their focus—even though they were ahead. The coach told the players the pitcher was the only team member still working. He said fielders were not standing in their ready positions, they were not talking or yelling out plays, and that they seemed to be waiting and hoping for the game to end rather than doing the things that put them on top in the game. That coach, like most others, wouldn't accept a lack of effort no matter what stage the game was in.

The ability to play the game "one pitch at a time" is a true characteristic of mental toughness. In softball, the fast action may last ten to fifteen seconds, followed by several minutes of slowdown or inactivity. The team that can stay mentally focused during the slow time in order to be sharp during the action is the team that most often comes out on top.

No matter how physically talented players are, coaches say, talent alone won't win games. The teams with the mental edge will be the teams playing in the post-season tournaments.

4 A Future in Fastpitch Softball

Whether girls pursue softball as a serious collegiate or professional sport or they remain weekend warriors in summer recreational leagues, they will benefit from competition and the team experience.

Meredith Shackleford started playing softball at an early age after discovering the game with her father. By the time she got to high school, her skills made her one of the top players in the country in 2000. And the lessons she learned on the field have enhanced her entire life. "Through softball, I have learned to be confident in most aspects of life. Being confident has helped me in school and to make new friends," she said. "I've also learned not to put much emphasis on day-to-day things but to look at the overall picture."

Participating in team sports helps provide valuable lessons for coping with situations

Participating in softball helps girls learn how to be competitive, work as a team, and strive with others to achieve a common goal.

outside of sports. Athletes learn how to work as a team, how to get along with others reaching for a common goal, how to win and loose gracefully, and the value of hard work. Through participation in sports, girls learn self-discipline, build self-confidence, and develop skills to handle competitive situations. These are qualities they will need as adults in dealing with friends, relationships, employers, and people in their communities.

Research conducted in 1991 by Skip Dane of Hardiness Research, Casper, Wyoming, revealed the following about participation in high school sports:

- Girls who participate in sports are three times more likely to do well in school than girls who do not.

- About 92 percent of sports participants do not use drugs.

- School athletes are more self-assured.

- Sports participants tend to enroll in both average classes and above-average or college-level classes.

- Sports participants receive above-average grades and do above average on skill tests.

- Those in sports have knowledge of and use financial aid and have a better chance of finishing college.

- Students involved in athletics appear to switch focus from pursuing financial gain to instead seeking life accomplishments as a result of their participation.

A nationwide study by the Women's Sports Foundation indicated that athletes do better in the classroom, are more involved in school activity programs, and stay involved in the community after graduation. The study also revealed that high school athletic participation has a positive educational and social impact on many minority and female students.

While the studies are clear—girls benefit from sports participation—the road to opportunity has taken a while. But now, nearly seven decades from the time gym teachers wanted girls to play softball so they wouldn't exert themselves too much, girls from grade school to high school, college, and beyond can't imagine not being able to play simply because of their gender.

"When I was very little, I got a Wiffle ball and bat for Christmas. I played with it every day. I even broke out one of our basement windows. Softball is so fun. It's a dirty game and I love playing it," said Michelle McCrady, who played from childhood through high school and into college in 2000.

McCrady and other girls have more opportunity than ever before to continue playing past high school. To measure the growing interest in the game, one need look no further than the number of colleges in the United States adding the sport to their varsity programs.

Since the fastpitch game became an official NCAA sport in 1982, the number of educational institutions sponsoring the sport has grown at a steady rate. In 1982 there were 143 Division I collegiate teams, no teams in Divisions II or III, 243 junior college teams, and 7,569 high school teams. Ten years later, in 1992, there were 1,119 collegiate teams in all divisions and 9,015 high school teams. In 1999, all levels of college teams fielded 1,423 teams and high school sponsored 12,679 teams.

Fastpitch softball ranks as the fourth most popular high school sport for girls, surpassed only by basketball, outdoor

This is the 2000 Women's U.S. Olympic softball gold medal team and its coaches.

track and field, and volleyball. In the 1998–1999 school year, fastpitch softball attracted 340,480 girls to play on high school teams.

The growth of the fastpitch game began with Title IX but continued to flourish with the success of the U.S. Olympic team in 1996—the first year the sport was in the Olympics—and 2000. Prior to the 1996 Olympics, the national team toured a half dozen U.S. cities to introduce the sport's players and build excitement for the games. When the national team and U.S. practice team played in the Midwest, thousands of fans turned out to watch the action, filling stadiums and every inch of grass behind the outfield in many cases. While many people attended out of curiosity, once fans got to see the fast-paced action, they were quickly won over.

Perhaps the biggest compliment for the sport came when a male reporter voiced his amazement at the game, and acknowledged he could not compete with the girls. "I was impressed by the outstanding overall athleticism, and especially enamored of the pitching. I saw rising fastball after rising fastball (interspersed with the occasional knee-buckling change-up) rocketing homeward and thought to myself, 'There is no way on God's green earth I could hit that,'" he wrote.

The reaction wasn't unusual as new fans told sports leaders they wanted more. The support resulted in the Women's Pro Softball League, which now runs every summer and is televised nationally on sports networks.

Sheila Douty, another Olympian, said attendance at exhibition games proved how popular the game was becoming. "It's just booming. The growth has been phenomenal. I was a physical therapist before, but I've been able to play ball full-time for a while now. We get endorsements. The pro league has started. To be able to go out and play every day and basically pay your bills is such a great feeling, and the majority of the players do that."

Dot Richardson, an Olympian and surgeon notes, "Even though some women play baseball, softball is still the avenue for girls who love to hold a glove and throw a ball and rip the cover off of it."

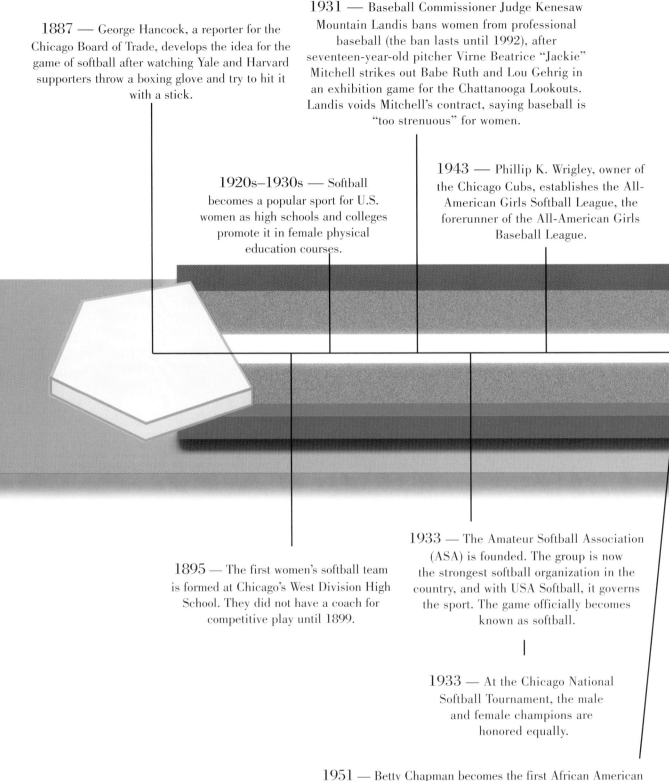

1887 — George Hancock, a reporter for the Chicago Board of Trade, develops the idea for the game of softball after watching Yale and Harvard supporters throw a boxing glove and try to hit it with a stick.

1931 — Baseball Commissioner Judge Kenesaw Mountain Landis bans women from professional baseball (the ban lasts until 1992), after seventeen-year-old pitcher Virne Beatrice "Jackie" Mitchell strikes out Babe Ruth and Lou Gehrig in an exhibition game for the Chattanooga Lookouts. Landis voids Mitchell's contract, saying baseball is "too strenuous" for women.

1920s–1930s — Softball becomes a popular sport for U.S. women as high schools and colleges promote it in female physical education courses.

1943 — Phillip K. Wrigley, owner of the Chicago Cubs, establishes the All-American Girls Softball League, the forerunner of the All-American Girls Baseball League.

1895 — The first women's softball team is formed at Chicago's West Division High School. They did not have a coach for competitive play until 1899.

1933 — The Amateur Softball Association (ASA) is founded. The group is now the strongest softball organization in the country, and with USA Softball, it governs the sport. The game officially becomes known as softball.

1933 — At the Chicago National Softball Tournament, the male and female champions are honored equally.

1951 — Betty Chapman becomes the first African American professional softball player as an outfielder on the Admiral Music Maids of the National Girls Baseball League of Chicago.

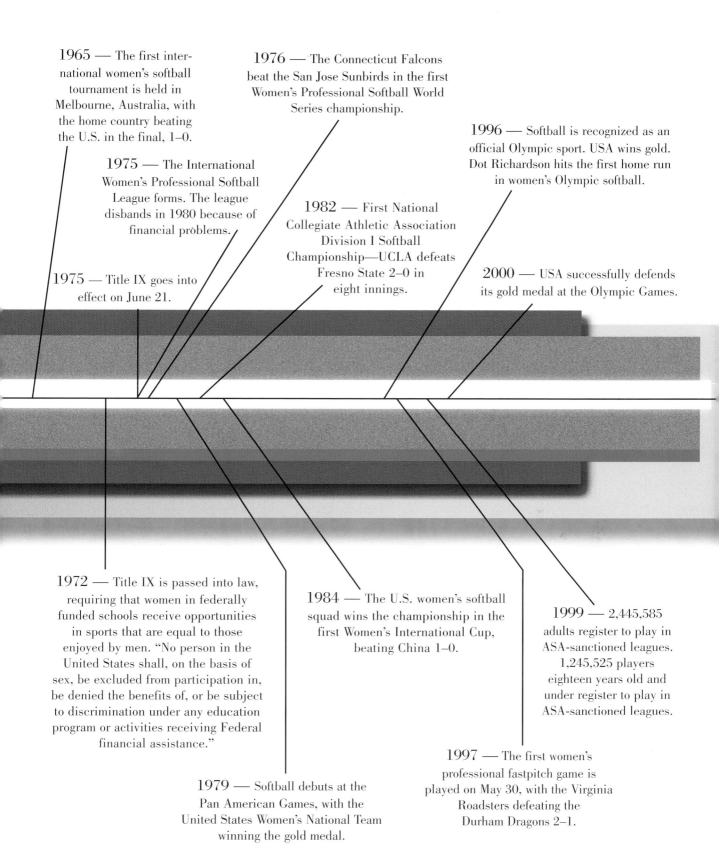

1965 — The first international women's softball tournament is held in Melbourne, Australia, with the home country beating the U.S. in the final, 1–0.

1976 — The Connecticut Falcons beat the San Jose Sunbirds in the first Women's Professional Softball World Series championship.

1996 — Softball is recognized as an official Olympic sport. USA wins gold. Dot Richardson hits the first home run in women's Olympic softball.

1975 — The International Women's Professional Softball League forms. The league disbands in 1980 because of financial problems.

1982 — First National Collegiate Athletic Association Division I Softball Championship—UCLA defeats Fresno State 2–0 in eight innings.

2000 — USA successfully defends its gold medal at the Olympic Games.

1975 — Title IX goes into effect on June 21.

1972 — Title IX is passed into law, requiring that women in federally funded schools receive opportunities in sports that are equal to those enjoyed by men. "No person in the United States shall, on the basis of sex, be excluded from participation in, be denied the benefits of, or be subject to discrimination under any education program or activities receiving Federal financial assistance."

1984 — The U.S. women's softball squad wins the championship in the first Women's International Cup, beating China 1–0.

1999 — 2,445,585 adults register to play in ASA-sanctioned leagues. 1,245,525 players eighteen years old and under register to play in ASA-sanctioned leagues.

1979 — Softball debuts at the Pan American Games, with the United States Women's National Team winning the gold medal.

1997 — The first women's professional fastpitch game is played on May 30, with the Virginia Roadsters defeating the Durham Dragons 2–1.

Glossary

backing up   A defensive player moves behind a teammate to field the ball in case of an error or in case the ball gets past the first player.

bag   The base.

base on balls   Batter receives four balls in one turn at bat and may advance to first base. Also called a walk.

bases full   Runners on first, second, and third base. Also called bases loaded.

batting average   Divide the total number of hits a batter has made by the total number of times at bat.

behind in the count   A batter is behind in the count when she has more strikes than balls. A pitcher is behind on the count when she has more balls than strikes.

bunt   A legally hit ball that is not swung at, but rather tapped slowly within the infield.

change-up   A straight pitch that goes over the plate at about two-thirds the speed of a fastball.

choking up   Moving your hands up on the bat handle—toward the barrel of the bat—to increase control.

cleanup   The fourth hitter in the batting order. This is usually the best hitter, batting in this position to get a hit allowing base runners to score.

count   The number of balls and strikes.

curve ball   A pitch that spins in a sideways rotation and will break to the right or left as it goes over the plate.

designated hitter   A hitter designated to bat for any one starting player.

double play   When two base runners are called out on the same play.

drop pitch   Pitch that breaks downward as it crosses over the plate, causing batters to swing over it.

earned run   A run that scores as a result of an offensive play, not because of an error by the defense.

earned run average (ERA)   The number of earned runs a pitcher averages per game. The number of earned runs divided by the number of innings pitched.

fastball   The most common pitch in softball. A straight pitch thrown as fast as possible with a forward rotation.

fielder's choice   The defensive team makes a play to put out a base runner rather than the batter.

force out   An out on a base runner who had to advance because the batter needed to occupy a base.

foul ball   A ball batted outside of fair territory.

full count   Three balls and two strikes on the batter.

grand slam   A home run with the bases loaded.

hit and run   An offensive strategy in which the batter hits and a base runner steals on the pitch.

hole   An area in the field that is not being covered by a defensive player.

infield   Fair territory within the base paths.

inning   The segment of a game where each team has a turn at bat and in which there are three outs for each team.

inside pitch   A pitched ball that misses the strike zone on the side near the batter.

knuckleball   A pitch that floats in the air but can move in any direction with the wind. Pitch has no rotation.

line drive   A ball that travels in a straight line close to the ground.

on deck   The next person to bat.

opposite field   The opposite field is the left side of the field for a right-handed batter, and the right side of the diamond for a left-handed batter.

outfield   The fair territory beyond the infield.

overthrow   To throw above or beyond a base person's or fielder's reach.

perfect game   A game in which the pitcher allows no hits and no runs, and where no opposing player gets on base. Extremely rare.

pinch hitter   A player sent into the game to hit in place of another batter.

pinch runner   A player sent into the game to run in place of another runner.

pop up   A short, high fly in or near the infield.

RBI   Run batted in.

rise pitch   A pitch that breaks upward as it crosses the plate, causing batters to swing under it.

sacrifice   Advancing a runner by forcing a play on the batter. For example, the batter will hit a fly ball to the outfield, knowing it will most likely be caught for an out, but that it will allow the base runner to advance.

shutout A game in which one team fails to score.

squeeze Bringing a runner home from third by bunting.

stealing A base runner trying to advance to the next base as the pitcher throws the ball to the batter.

strike zone Any area above home plate between the batter's knees and armpits when using a normal batting stance.

tag up On a long fly, the runner goes back to the bag, and then runs to the next base after the ball is touched by a fielder.

walk When a batter has four balls called, and may advance safely to first base.

windmill A pitching delivery in which the pitcher's arm moves in a circle starting in front of the body, swinging over the head and ending just after the hand and arm pass the hips.

For More Information

National Fastpitch Coaches Association
409 Vandiver Drive, Suite 5-202
Columbia, MO 65202
(573) 875-3033
Web site: http://www.nfca.org

Women's Sports Foundation
Eisenhower Park
East Meadow, NY 11554
(516) 542-4700
(800) 227-3988
Web site:
http://www.WomenSportsFoundation.org

Web Sites

Amateur Softball Association of America (ASA)
Web site: http://www.softball.org
The ASA, which is the national governing body of softball, is primarily responsible for providing structured leagues for nearly four million players, coaches, and umpires. The ASA establishes uniform softball rules and regulations and provides instruction in the game to both coaches and players. Visit the local contacts and Web sites page to find information specific to your state and city.

NCAA Softball
Web site: http://www.ncaasoftball.com/
News, standings, and information about Division I, II, and III collegiate softball.

SoftballSearch.com
Web site: http://www.softballsearch.com
This is an on-line community designed to connect players, coaches, teams, leagues, and families to softball.

Women's Pro Softball League
Web site: http://www.prosoftball.com
Official site of the WPSL, with links to member teams, news, and information.

For Further Reading

Babb, Ron. *Etched in Gold: The Story of America's First-Ever Olympic Gold Medal Winning Softball Team.* Indianapolis, IN: Masters Press, 1997.

Brill, Marlene Targ. *Winning Women in Baseball and Softball.* Hauppauge, NY: Barron's, 2000.

Elliott, Jill, and Martha Ewing, eds. *Youth Softball: A Complete Handbook.* Dubuque, IA: Brown and Benchmark, 1992.

Hastings, Penny. *Sports for Her: A Reference Guide for Teenage Girls.* Westport, CT: Greenwood Publishing Group, 1999.

Joseph, Jacquie. *Defensive Softball Drills.* Champaign, IL: Human Kinetics Publishing, 1998.

Linde, Karen, and Robert G. Hoehn. *Girls' Softball: A Complete Guide for Players and Coaches.* West Nyack, NY: Parker Publishing, 1985.

Monteleone, John, and Deborah Crisfield. *The Louisville Slugger Complete Book of Women's Fast-Pitch Softball.* New York: Henry Holt and Co., 1999.

Pasternak, Ceel, and Linda Thornburg. *Cool Careers for Girls in Sports.* Manassas Park, VA: Impact Publications, 1998.

Potter, Diane L., and Gretchen A. Brockmeyer. *Softball: Steps to Success.* 2nd ed. Champaign, IL: Human Kinetics Publishing, 1999.

Richardson, Dot, and Don Yaeger. *Living the Dream.* New York: Kensington Books, 1997.

Roberts, Robin. *Careers for Women Who Love Sports.* Brookfield, CT: Millbrook Press, 2000.

Sammons, Barry E. *Fastpitch Softball: The Windmill Pitcher.* Indianapolis, IN: Masters Press, 1997.

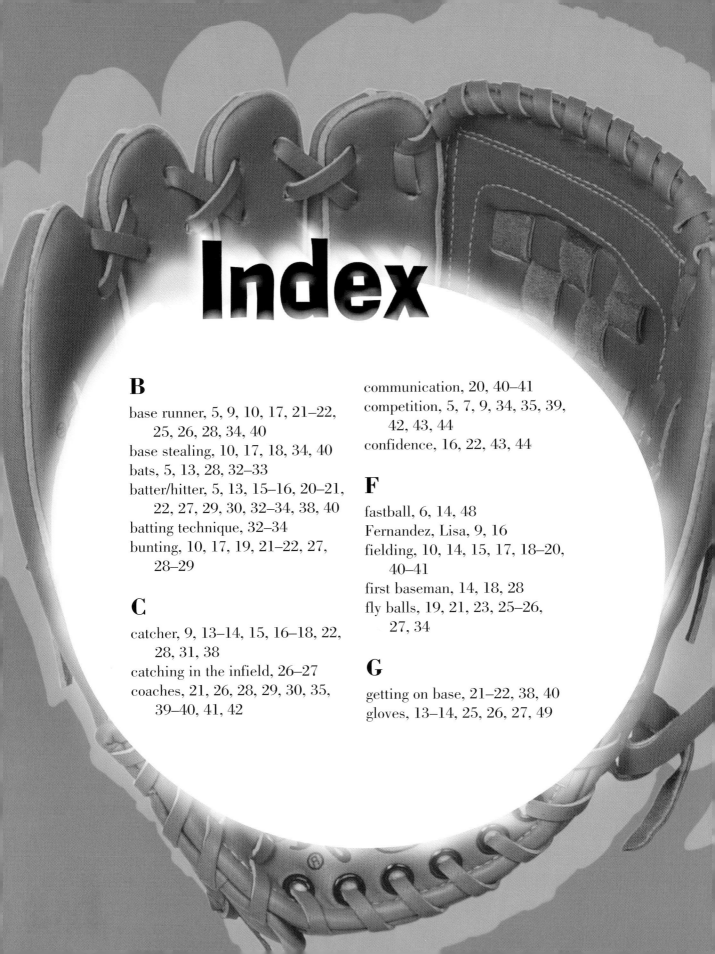

Index

About the Author

Ann Wesley lives and works in Bloomington, Indiana, and is an avid sports fan. She has a degree in journalism from Indiana University, and has written for newspapers and magazines. Wesley currently works as a director of a Web design company.

Credits

Cover photo by Maura Boruchow; pp. 3, 5, 8, 9, 10, 11, 23, 32, 35, 43, 52, 53, 55, 57–63 by Cindy Reiman; pp. 4, 50–51 by Tom Forget; p. 6 © Underwood & Underwood/Corbis; p. 12 © FPG/Michael Hart, 1988; p. 15 and 16 by Maura Boruchow; p. 17 © Corbis; p. 19 © Associated Press/The Journal; p. 24 © FPG/Jim Cummins, 1998; p. 29 © O.J. Callahan/The Sun Sentinel; p. 31 © Jonathan Blair/Corbis; p. 37 © Duomo/Corbis; p. 39 © AllSport USA; p. 44 © James Marshall/Corbis; p. 47 © AllSport USA.

Series Design and Layout

Danielle Goldblatt